My Gullah Kitchen

Eva Segar

Eva Segar

Please direct all correspondence and book orders to:
Mrs. Eva Segar
104 Community Center Road
Seabrook, S.C. 29940
Phone: 843-846-4697

ISBN: 0-9769229-4-0

Published by

www.BarbaraMartin.net
Y O U   S H O U L D   W R I T E   A   B O O K

Beaufort, S.C.
843-263-5248
E-mail: barbara@barbaramartin.net

Photos supplied by the author, except where photo credits indicate.
Cover design by Barbara Martin

First Edition

To all the great cooks
whose food I have eaten
and whose recipes I have read
and whose stories I have heard.

Acknowledgements

Many of the recipes in this book
were given to me over the years
or demonstrated for me in my kitchen
by family and friends.
To all I am grateful.
Special thanks to my grandmother
Louise Smalls,
my mother Florence Smalls,
and my aunt Elizabeth Williams.
I thank my entire family
for trusting me in the kitchen.

A Word to the Reader

It's not easy to take a recipe handed down from generation to generation and turn it into a formula that everybody can understand and follow. How do you translate "a palm full" of this or "just a touch" of that? I'm not a trained chef, but I am a homemaker, a farmer's daughter and a farmer's wife. I'm good at taking what the sea, the fields, the ponds and rivers, and even the woods offer and turning it, without a lot of fuss or expense, into simple, filling food. I've done my best to make these recipes understandable to someone who's never stood in my mother's kitchen and watched her cook. Most recipes are just general guidelines anyway, and you can make these your own by adding your own favorite ingredients.

Servings per recipe will vary, too, depending on your family's appetite. Obviously, a man who comes in from the fields is going to be a lot hungrier than a man who spent his day behind a desk.

I've divided this cookbook into unusual categories: From the Pantry, From the Field and Garden, From the Water, From the Woods, etc. That's because my family has always lived on the bounty of the land and the sea that surrounded us, and because the pantry—even in hard times—held flour and cornmeal and other staples that allowed us to make mouth-watering cakes and breads.

Foreword

I learned to cook from my grandmother, Louise Smalls, and my mother, Florence Smalls. They allowed me to "play cook" in the kitchen and watch them.

One day, Mother came home and said, "Sister, you was home all day. How come you didn't put on the rice? And why didn't you boil the beans or peas or something?" So I went from "play cooking" to cooking for ten or more people just about every day. I've been cooking ever since.

On the Fourth of July, we always invited family members and friends. We would have a little cookout, with hot dogs and hamburgers, French fries, and soda to drink. We also cooked soul food: collard greens, string beans, butter beans, fried chicken, macaroni and cheese, corn bread, and red rice. We all ate so much food every Fourth of July. Then we'd start drinking and dancing, and that's what we did for the rest of the day. It was always a good day.

Because we lived in South Carolina's lowcountry, rice was the central part of almost every family meal. A person didn't think they had eaten a full meal unless rice was included. We loved a meal of rice, corn bread and beans. That meal made us fat because we went to sleep after we ate it. My grandmother used to say, "Eat something that sticks to your ribs." And my mother always said we had to have rice to eat because we worked hard on the farm and we had to have something to give us strength. We ate grits, like every other Southern family, but only in the morning. When dinner time came, we had to have that rice.

I remember picking beans in the field on our farm in Beaufort County's Dale community. Farming wasn't an easy life back then, but life is better today because my family and I worked hard to get where we are. None of us minded the hard work, though. I was brought up that way. We were taught to never be idle, never waste time. It was a way of thinking that was passed on from my grandmother to my mother, and she, in turn, passed it down to me.

When I was a girl, most of what we ate was either grown on

our farm or was traded for something someone else grew on theirs. Still, we had all kinds of wonderful things to eat. In the summer, we ate fresh sweet corn and tomatoes, tiny green beans, tender young greens, baby limas, and other mouth-watering fresh vegetables. We had butter beans of all colors and plenty of fresh-picked field peas, which we ate fresh with their snaps. If you've never had field peas and snaps, I'm sorry to say that you have passed a great treat. You'd eat the snaps and the peas together after cooking them in water with a little bit of salt pork or ham. They were so delicious; it makes my mouth water just to think about them.

A lot of people call field peas "cow peas." That's because after we did all our picking in the pea fields, we let our cows in to graze. That way, nothing was wasted.

We ate as many of the fresh field peas as we could, and the rest would be dried and stored in cloth sacks for the winter. But before we could dry them, we had to shell them. This would have taken a long time if it weren't for a certain trick: You'd place the peas in a croker sack, then beat them with a stick to loosen the shell. Then you'd hold a dishpan of peas up high over your head and slowly drop them on a sheet on the ground. The wind would push the shells away from the peas as they fell. You could do this only on a windy day.

When I was coming up, we never put fertilizer in our crops to rush up the food. Food used to taste much better than what you can get in the supermarket today, and I think all the chemicals used in the fields now cause health problems. I guess a lot of people agree with me because a lot of young people now want to buy food as fresh as you can get from the fields, and they're willing to pay a lot for it. But in my day, fresh food wasn't a luxury; we survived on it.

My favorite thing in the kitchen is baking. There's nothing as good as a homemade cake or pie, sometimes still just a little warm from the oven. They make the whole house smell good, and that smell calls my husband in from the fields with a smile on his face.

That's why there are a good many recipes for pies and cakes in this book.

It wasn't always easy to put down measurements because every good cook knows how to throw together a little bit of this and a little bit of that, a handful of this and a pinch of that. When you've made the same cake a hundred times, and you watched your mother and your grandmother make the same cake before you, you don't really need a measuring spoon. But I've done my best to get the measurements for these heirloom recipes right and make them easy to follow.

I hope your kitchen smells so good, your family comes to the table with smiles on their faces.

Recipes

My Gullah Kitchen

From the Field and Garden

A head of cabbage from my garden will be in the pot shortly. The fresher the food, the better tasting—and the better for you, I believe.

The Best Black-Eyed Peas

Along with collard greens, black-eyed peas are traditionally served on New Year's Day to bring good luck. The legend is that anyone who eats the peas will have plenty of coin to spend in the year to come.

1 16-ounce package dried black-eyed peas
1 medium onion, studded with 8 to 10 whole cloves
4 cloves of garlic
1 cup minced red bell pepper
1 teaspoon red pepper flakes
¼ pound country ham, chopped
4 10½-ounce cans of chicken broth (or make your own, which is even better)
¼ cup to ½ cup water, if needed toward the end of cooking time.

Rinse the peas in a bowl, changing the water two or three times. Remove any bits of debris and peas that float to the top. Place the peas, clove-studded onion, garlic, bell pepper, pepper flakes and ham in a slow cooker. Cover with chicken broth and cook on low, stirring every hour until the peas are done and the liquid is creamy and slightly thickened. If the liquid becomes too thick, add enough water to thin to the desired consistency. Remove the cloves. Serve over fluffy white rice.
Makes 6 to 8 servings.

String Beans with Smoked Turkey and White Potatoes

If preparing fresh green beans is too much trouble, by all means substitute three bags of frozen green beans. You can also substitute ham or bacon for the turkey. The sugar in this recipe brings out the natural sweetness of string beans. Cook the beans just until tender to keep the bright green color.

1 cup smoked turkey, cut into bite-size pieces
3 pounds fresh, whole string beans
¼ teaspoon sugar
2 large, white potatoes, peeled, cubed and parboiled
salt and pepper to taste

Bring 6 quarts of water to a boil in a covered pot. Add the turkey and continue to boil, with the lid off, for about 10 minutes. Sprinkle the sugar over the beans and add them to the pot. Add the potatoes and cook another 10 to 20 minutes. Taste for seasoning and add salt and pepper as needed.
Makes 8 servings.

Stewed Cabbage with Potatoes

Cabbage is sweet and filling when it isn't overcooked. Serve it as a side dish with pork chops. If summer savory is not available, use a tablespoon of chopped, fresh mint and a tablespoon of chopped, fresh thyme.

1 large head of cabbage
2 large potatoes, peeled and cut in large chunks
1 teaspoon salt
3 teaspoons dried summer savory, divided

Cut the cabbage into quarters and soak it in a bowl of salted water. In the meantime, bring 5 quarts of water to a boil in a large pot. Add the cabbage, potatoes, salt and 2 teaspoons of the summer savory. Cook until the potatoes are tender. Drain and toss with the rest of the summer savory.
Makes 4 to 6 servings.

How to get greens ready for the pot

If your greens are fresh from the garden, you're going to have to do a little work before you can throw them in the pot. First, you have to pick them over to make sure no bugs or caterpillars are hidden in the leaves. Then you want to start the process of getting the grit off the leaves. My mother always slapped each leaf against the palm of her hand to shake free as much of the sand as possible before she even bothered to wash them. You want to soak the leaves in a sink full (or dishpan full) of cold water, changing the water several times. Then you pull off and discard any thick stems and tear the leaves into pieces about the size of the palm of your hand. At this point, it wouldn't hurt to rinse the leaves in cold water one more time and then they're finally ready for the pot! If you're thinking it takes a lot of work to get the greens from garden to plate, you're right. But greens are a cool-weather crop, and we had greens and cabbage growing in the garden when everything else had gone to seed. A big bowl of greens served with corn bread to soak up the pot likker is some of the best eatin' you can imagine on a fall night.

Collard Greens with Smoked Turkey Wings

Collards are better if they are picked after the first frost, and there's no better eatin' when you serve them with cracklin corn bread. (Recipe is on page 55.)

2 smoked turkey wings
3 bunches collards
1 sweet onion, chopped
2 hot red peppers
1 tablespoon sugar
salt and pepper to taste

Pick over the greens and wash them. Chop the leaves coarsely. Discard any large, tough stems. In a large pot, cover the turkey wings with water and boil for an hour. Pick out the wings, chop the meat off the bones, and return the meat to the pot, along with the collards, onion, and seasonings. Simmer the collards for about 1½ hours, adding water as needed.

Collard Greens with Pork

You have to cook collards longer than other greens. You want them very tender. Leftover greens are delicious reheated in a frying pan with crushed red pepper.

½ pound smoked pork neck bones
about 3 pieces of pig tails or 3 pieces of fresh neck bones
5 pounds greens
1 dried hot pepper (optional)

Boil the smoked pork in about a gallon of water, uncovered, for about 30 minutes. What you're looking for here is a nice, rich broth. In the meantime, clean the collard greens. You'll end up with only about 3 pounds of greens, since the stems of the collards are tough and must be thrown away. Tear the greens into pieces about the size of your palm and add them to the pot along with the hot pepper. Simmer the greens, uncovered, until they're tender, up to 2 hours. Serve with hot pepper vinegar.
Makes 10 to 12 servings.

Turnips

Serve this with hot pepper vinegar.

¼ pound side meat (salt pork)
2 medium bunches of turnips with their greens, cleaned and chopped
1 pound smoked ham hocks
salt and pepper to taste

In a large pot, cover the meat with water and simmer for about an hour, until the ham hocks begin to fall off the bone. Add the turnip greens and seasonings and simmer for 15 minutes. Add the chopped turnip root and simmer another 15 minutes or until the roots are tender.
Makes 4 servings.

Okra Soup

Okra is harvested toward the end of the summer. It's very easy to grow, and just about everybody who's Southern loves okra. Rice or corn bread go good with okra soup.

1 large, meaty beef shank bone
3 pounds okra, trimmed and cut into small pieces
3 pounds fresh tomatoes, peeled and chopped (canned tomatoes can be substituted)
1 large onion, chopped
1 bay leaf
a fresh thyme sprig
½ teaspoon salt

Place the shank in a large stock pot and cover with about 3 quarts of water. Bring to a boil, reduce the heat and simmer, uncovered, for 2 hours or until the meat is tender. Add the okra, tomatoes, onion, herbs, and salt and cook for another 1½ hours.

Steamed Okra

Trim the okra pods just where the stem begins, but don't cut into the pods. Put a tiny bit of water, a few tablespoons, into a pan, add the okra and cover, making sure you have a tight fit. Steam the okra over medium-high heat for about 10 minutes or until all the water evaporates. Open the lid and dress the okra with a bit of butter and salt and pepper.

Okra Pickles

Okra pickles are my favorite. If you can't grow your own okra, try to find very fresh pods that haven't been damaged in the picking. You want your pods all about the same size, about the size of your pointin' finger. Each pound of okra will yield two pints of pickles.

3 pounds small, young okra pods
12 garlic cloves, peeled
6 to 12 fresh hot peppers
1 tablespoon mustard seeds (you'll use about a ½ teaspoon of mustard seeds for each jar of pickles)
3 cups water
¼ cup salt
6 cups white vinegar

Wash the okra and trim the ends off the stems, but don't cut into the pod. Pack the whole pods tightly in the jars, alternating stem end up, then stem end down. Divide the garlic, peppers, and mustard seeds among the jars. Bring the water, salt, and vinegar to a boil and pour over the okra to within ½ inch of the rims. Place a lid and ring on each jar. Lower the jars into a canning kettle and process for 10 minutes at a full boil. Remove the jars from the water and set them aside to cool. Check to be sure each lid has sealed. Tighten the bands and store the pickles for one month before eating.

Okra and Tomatoes

This simple dish of stewed tomatoes and okra is served over rice alongside pork, poultry, or seafood. Don't salt the stew. The bacon will impart its salty smokiness to the vegetables.

8 thick slices hickory-smoked bacon
1 medium onion, chopped
1 pound fresh okra, trimmed and sliced
5 vine-ripened tomatoes, peeled and quartered, or a large can (1 ½ pounds) of whole, peeled tomatoes, quartered, with their juice
1 fresh hot pepper or cayenne pepper to taste

Cook the bacon in a cast iron skillet over medium heat until it's crisp. Set aside the bacon to drain, and add the onion. Cook the onion in the bacon grease until it softens and looks translucent, about five minutes. Add the okra and continue cooking until the okra begins to glisten with moisture. Add the tomatoes and pepper and lower the heat. Simmer, uncovered, until the okra and tomatoes are tender. Be careful not to overcook the okra. It should be tender but still bright green. Serve over white rice.
Makes 4 to 6 servings.

Okra Gumbo

1½ cups okra, trimmed and sliced
½ cup onion, chopped
½ cup green pepper, chopped
1 can of tomatoes
about 2 tablespoons fat for frying
1 tablespoon sugar
1 teaspoon flour
¾ teaspoon salt
¼ teaspoon pepper

Cook the okra in a small amount of water for 10 minutes. Drain.
Fry the onion and pepper in a small amount of fat until tender, not
brown. Blend in the sugar, flour and seasonings. Add tomatoes and
okra. Cook over low heat until hot, about 15 minutes.
Makes 4 to 6 servings.

Eva's Vegetable Creole

1 quart shredded cabbage
2 cups sliced celery
3 tomatoes, diced
1 cup green pepper, chopped
½ cup onions, chopped
3 tablespoon butter
1 teaspoon salt
pinch of pepper

Melt butter in a skillet. Add remaining ingredients. Cover and cook slowly about 12 minutes or until the vegetables are crisp but tender.
Makes 6 to 8 servings.

Fried Summer Squash

5 yellow squash, sliced
1 tablespoon oil
1 tablespoon butter
1 cup diced onions
salt and black pepper to taste
1 teaspoon fresh rosemary leaves, finely chopped

In a large skillet, fry the squash in oil and butter. When they're just slightly brown, add the onions. Season with salt and pepper. Cook over medium heat until the onions are softened, but do not allow the squash to become mushy. Sprinkle with rosemary and keep warm until you're ready to serve.
Makes 4 servings.

Squash Casserole

3 cups cooked yellow squash
½ cup cracker crumbs
1 can undiluted mushroom soup
1 egg, slightly beaten
1 tablespoon minced onion
½ cup shredded cheese
½ teaspoon salt
¼ teaspoon pepper
Mix all ingredients and pour into a casserole dish. Bake for 40 minutes at 350 degrees.
Makes 6 to 8 servings.

Broccoli and Cauliflower Salad

1 head cauliflower, chopped small
1 bunch broccoli, chopped small
½ a large red onion
⅓ cup sour cream
½ cup mayonnaise
garlic salt

Sprinkle a good bit of garlic salt over the broccoli and cauliflower. Store in the refrigerator overnight. Next morning, add the onion, sour cream, and mayonnaise. Mix well and let stand in the refrigerator 6 to 8 hours.
Makes 4 to 6 servings.

Potato Salad

6 cups peeled, diced, cooked potatoes
1 medium onion, finely chopped
1 cup finely diced celery
1 cup chopped dill pickles
1 cup sweet relish, drained
8 large hard-boiled eggs, 4 chopped, 4 left whole
salt and black pepper to taste
1½ cups mayonnaise
fresh parsley, chopped

Combine potatoes, onion, celery, pickles and chopped eggs. Season with salt and pepper and add mayonnaise. Chill several hours. Just before serving, cut the 4 remaining eggs in half and place them on the potato salad as decoration and dust the salad with parsley. Serve at once.
Makes 6 to 8 servings.

Sweet Potato Pone

4 cups grated raw sweet potatoes
2 cups molasses or dark corn syrup
1 cup brown sugar
1 teaspoon cinnamon
¼ cup raisins
1 cup warm water
1 cup chopped citron
grated rind of 1 orange
grated rind of 1 lemon
1 teaspoon chopped or powdered ginger
2 tablespoons coconut (optional)

Mix ingredients and pour into a greased rectangular baking dish. Bake in a moderate oven (350 degrees) until a nice crust forms on top, about an hour. Serve hot with unsweetened cream, plain or whipped.

Sweet Potato Casserole

3 cups cooked, mashed sweet potatoes
3 eggs, well beaten
1 teaspoon vanilla
1 stick butter, melted
Mix all the ingredients listed above and pour into a casserole dish. Add topping (recipe follows) and bake at 350 degrees for 30 minutes.

Topping:

⅓ cup butter
⅔ cup brown sugar
⅓ cup flour
1 cup nuts (pecans or walnuts)
1 cup coconut

Melt butter and add sugar. Stir until dissolved. Stir in flour, nuts, and coconut. Sprinkle on top of casserole before baking.

From the Pantry

Here I am in my kitchen, baking up a storm for a family reunion.

Eva's Nut Cake

Pecan trees are abundant in this part of the country and are as common as seafood in the Gullah kitchen. When I was a child, we knew that as long as we had flour and sugar in the pantry, butter and milk from our cows, and eggs from our chickens, we could always make dessert.

1 pound cake flour
1 pound sugar
½ pound butter
6 eggs
⅓ cup milk
¼ cup sherry
1 quart (or more) chopped pecans
1 teaspoon nutmeg
1 teaspoon baking powder

Preheat the oven to 350 degrees. Cream butter and sugar. Add eggs, one at a time. Add flour, nutmeg, baking power and milk. Add sherry and fold in pecans. Bake in moderate (350 degrees) oven for 2 hours.

Old Fashioned Cream Pie

1 stick butter
1 cup sugar
2¼ cups milk, divided (or replace 1 cup of the milk with 1 cup
heavy cream for a richer filling)
¼ cup cornstarch
1 baked pie shell
nutmeg

Preheat the oven to 400 degrees. Heat 2 cups of the milk, the sugar,
and the butter in the top of a double boiler, stirring frequently, until
the milk is very hot, the sugar is dissolved, and the butter is melted.
Stir the cornstarch into the remaining ¼ cup of milk until it's free
of lumps. Add to the hot milk mixture. Continue to cook about 5
minutes, stirring constantly, until the mixture has thickened. Pour
into a baked pie shell. Sprinkle with the nutmeg and bake at 400
degrees about 5 minutes.

Apple Pie Filling

7½ cups sliced apples
⅓ cup brown sugar, firmly packed
1 teaspoon cinnamon
⅓ teaspoon nutmeg
¼ cup lemon juice
½ cup cornstarch
1¾ cups white sugar
¾ teaspoon salt
2 tablespoons butter

Preheat the oven to 425 degrees. Mix cornstarch, brown sugar, white sugar, cinnamon, nutmeg, and salt. Sprinkle the lemon juice over the apples and then toss the apples with the sugar mixture. Place the apples in your pie crust and dot with butter. Add the top crust and crimp closed. Cut steam vents in the top crust and bake at 400 degrees for 40 minutes.

Sweet Potato Pie

Holiday dinners wouldn't be complete without an old-fashioned potato pie. Most people like them best at room temperature or even a little bit warm with whipped cream.

5 large baked sweet potatoes, peeled and mashed
4 large eggs
½ cup half-and-half
1 cup sugar
1 teaspoon vanilla
¾ teaspoon nutmeg
½ teaspoon cinnamon
½ cup butter, melted
2 9-inch deep-dish pie crusts, unbaked

Preheat the oven to 350 degrees. Mix all the ingredients, divide them into the two pie crusts and bake 45 minutes to an hour, or until the filling is just set.

Peach Pie

Some people might call this a cobbler because of the unusual way the crust is made, but my family always considered it pie. No matter what you call it, it's delicious made with fresh, local peaches. You probably could substitute frozen peaches, but it wouldn't be the same.

1 stick butter or margarine
¾ cup sugar
1 cup milk
1 cup self-rising flour
1 quart peaches, peeled, pitted, and sliced
½ cup sour cream
1 teaspoon lemon extract

Preheat the oven to 350 degrees. Melt butter in a baking pan. Mix flour, sugar, milk, sour cream, and lemon extract in a bowl. Add the melted butter. Drain most of the juice off the peaches and add them to the buttered pan. Pour the batter evenly over the peaches. Bake for about 45 minutes, until the top is browned and the peaches are bubbly.

Sour Milk Ginger Cake

If you don't have sour milk, just mix in ½ teaspoon of vinegar or lemon juice to your sweet milk and allow it to sit for a few minutes.

¼ cup butter
½ cup sugar
1 egg, well beaten
½ cup molasses
1⅔ cups flour
½ teaspoon baking soda
1 teaspoon baking powder
1 teaspoon dried ginger
½ teaspoon salt
½ cup sour milk

Topping:

2 tablespoons sugar
1 teaspoon cinnamon

Preheat the oven to 350 degrees. Sift the flour, baking soda, baking powder, ginger, and salt together and set aside. Cream butter and sugar thoroughly. Add egg and molasses, beating well. Add the dry ingredients alternately with the milk and beat until smooth. Pour into a buttered, rectangular baking pan. Mix an additional 2 tablespoons of sugar and a teaspoon of cinnamon together and sprinkle on top of the cake. Bake in a moderate oven for 45 minutes.

Buttermilk Pie

For variation, you can leave out the lemon flavoring and add 1 can of flaked coconut.

1⅓ cups sugar
3 tablespoons flour
2 eggs
¼ cup melted margarine
1 cup thick buttermilk
2 teaspoons vanilla
1 teaspoon lemon flavoring
1 9-inch chilled pie shell

Preheat the oven to 425. Mix the sugar, flour, eggs, margarine and buttermilk. Fold in the flavorings, and pour the batter into a chilled 9-inch pie shell. Bake at 425 degrees for 10 minutes. Reduce heat to 350 and bake another 35 minutes without opening the oven door.

Baked Chocolate Pie

3 cups sugar
7 tablespoons unsweetened cocoa
¼ teaspoon salt
4 eggs
1 teaspoon vanilla
1 can evaporated milk
1 can coconut
2 unbaked pie shells

Preheat the oven to 350 degrees. Mix together sugar, cocoa, and salt. Stir in eggs, vanilla and milk. Add coconut and mix well. Pour into pie shells and bake for about 25 minutes, or until the center of the pie is almost set.

Squash Pie

Tastes like sweet potato pie.

2 cups cooked winter squash
⅓ cup evaporated milk
1 tablespoon cornstarch
3 tablespoons butter
1 teaspoon vanilla
4 eggs
1½ cups sugar
½ teaspoon salt
2 soda crackers, rolled fine
1 pie shell, unbaked

Preheat oven to 400 degrees. Mix together all the pie filling ingredients and pour into the pie shell. Bake at 400 degrees for 15 minutes, then bake at 375 for another 45 minutes.

Peach (or Apple) Cobbler

2 cups all-purpose flour
1 teaspoon baking powder
¾ teaspoon salt
3 tablespoons sugar
¼ cup shortening
¾ whipping cream
8 cups sliced fresh peaches or apples
2 cups sugar, plus more for sprinkling
2 tablespoons all-purpose flour
½ teaspoon ground cinnamon
1 teaspoon vanilla extract
⅓ cup butter or margarine

Combine first 4 ingredients. Cut in shortening until the mixture resembles coarse meal. Sprinkle with cream and toss with a fork until the dough comes together. Knead 4 or 5 times, wrap in plastic wrap, and chill at least an hour. Meanwhile, combine fruit, sugar, flour, and cinnamon in a Dutch oven. Set aside until a syrup forms. Then bring to a boil, reduce heat, and simmer, uncovered, 10 minutes or until the fruit is tender. Remove from heat and stir in vanilla and butter. Stir until the butter melts. Preheat the oven to 425 degrees. Roll half the chilled dough into a 12-by-8 inch rectangle. Spoon half the fruit into a lightly buttered 12-by-8-by-2 inch baking pan. Place the pastry on top, sprinkled with sugar, and bake for 15 minutes or until the crust is very light brown. Spoon remaining fruit on top, roll remaining pastry thin and cut into 1-inch strips. Arrange strips in a lattice design over the fruit and sprinkle with sugar. Bake 20 more minutes.

Grandmother Louise's Pound Cake

3 sticks butter
2 cups sugar
6 eggs
1 cup self-rising flour
2 cups all-purpose flour
2 teaspoons vanilla
2 teaspoons lemon extract
1 cup milk

Preheat oven to 350 degrees. Mix butter, sugar, and eggs well, then add all the other ingredients and mix well. Bake in a greased and floured Bundt pan for 1½ hours or until a wooden pick inserted in the center comes out clean. Cool 20 minutes and remove from the pan to cool completely.

Eggless, Butterless Cake

2 cups flour
1 cup sugar
1½ teaspoons soda
1 cup mayonnaise
1¼ teaspoons baking powder
4 tablespoons cocoa
1 cup cold water

Preheat oven to 350 degrees, and grease and flour 2 round cake pans. Blend all dry ingredients well. Mix mayonnaise and water and beat into the dry ingredients. Bake 30 minutes. Cool and frost with your favorite chocolate icing.

Grandma's Wacky Cake

This cake is mixed entirely in the pan that it's to be baked in. Grease the pan, dump in the ingredients, and mix together with a whisk or a wooden spoon. It's as simple as that.

2 cups sugar
3 cups all-purpose flour
1 teaspoon salt
½ cup unsweetened cocoa
2 teaspoons baking soda
2 tablespoons vinegar
⅔ cup oil
2 cups cold water
1 teaspoon vanilla

Preheat oven to 350 degrees. Mix all ingredients in a 12-by-9 inch baking pan until all lumps are gone. Bake 30 to 35 minutes.

Black Walnut Pound Cake

Black walnuts have a distinctive flavor. You cannot substitute other nuts or even an English walnut and get the same flavor.

1 cup butter
½ cup vegetable shortening
3 cups sugar
5 eggs
3 cups unsifted, all-purpose flour
1 teaspoon baking powder
¼ teaspoon salt
1 cup milk
1 teaspoon vanilla
1 teaspoon black walnut flavoring
1 cup chopped black walnuts

Preheat oven to 350. Cream butter, shortening, and sugar until fluffy. Add eggs, one at a time. Sift flour, baking powder, and salt together. Add the flour mixture alternately with the milk, beginning and ending with the flour. Stir in flavorings and nuts. Bake at 350 degrees for 10 minutes. Turn the oven down to 325 and bake for 1 hour, or until a wooden pick inserted in the middle of the cake comes out clean. Immediately turn the cake out of the pan and cool.

Eva's Chocolate Cake

You can sour the milk by adding ½ teaspoon vinegar or lemon juice and letting the milk stand for a few minutes.

1 egg
½ cup cocoa, plus extra for preparing the pans
½ cup melted shortening
1½ cups flour
1 cup sour milk
1 teaspoon baking soda
1 teaspoon salt
1 cup sugar
½ cup boiling water

Grease pans and coat with cocoa instead of flour. Put all the ingredients into a mixing bowl in the order they are listed. Don't stir until the boiling water goes in, then beat well. Bake in 2 prepared loaf pans or 2 8-inch round pans. Bake about 25 minutes (loaf pan may take longer than round pan) or until the center of the cake springs back when touched. Cool and frost with Eva's Mocha Frosting (recipe follows).

Eva's Mocha Frosting

½ cup soft butter
1½ cups sifted powdered sugar
1 tablespoons cocoa
very strong, cold coffee

Cream butter, cocoa, and sugar. Gradually add the coffee until the frosting is the desired consistency.

Here's how we shelled corn when I was a child.

Most of the recipes in this section have been desserts, but no recipe book would be complete without at least a mention of cornmeal. A farmhouse pantry always holds cornmeal because it's cheap and filling, and not many meals pass without some kind of corn bread showing up on my table. You might be surprised at all the ways you can cook cornmeal. Here are just a few.

Corn Muffins

Slather these sweet muffins with butter and you have a cheap treat that your family will love.

3 large eggs
1½ cups buttermilk
1 cup stone ground cornmeal
1 cup whole-wheat flour
¼ cup sugar
1 teaspoon salt
1 teaspoon baking power
1 teaspoon baking soda
½ cup creamed corn
¼ shredded cheddar cheese
1 tablespoon chopped jalapeno pepper
6 tablespoons melted butter

Preheat the oven to 400 degrees. Beat the eggs with the buttermilk in a large bowl. Add the cornmeal, flour, sugar, salt, baking powder and baking soda. Mix until just combined and stir in the corn, cheese and pepper. Add the melted butter and stir until all the ingredients are well combined. Pour the batter into a prepared muffin pan, filling each cup ¾ full. Bake 20 minutes or until the tops of the muffins are golden brown.

Cracklin Corn Bread

Cracklins are small pieces of salt pork that have been slowly fried until crisp and dry. They add flavor and crunch to the bread. Add a cold glass of buttermilk to drink, and this bread makes a satisfying breakfast.

2 cups white cornmeal
¼ cup sifted all-purpose flour
1 tablespoon sugar
½ teaspoon salt
4 teaspoons baking powder
1½ cups plus 2 tablespoons milk
2 large eggs, beaten well
2 tablespoons butter, melted
½ pound crisp cracklins, broken into half-inch pieces.

Preheat oven to 350 degrees. Grease an 8-inch square pan. Mix the dry ingredients. Stir in milk, eggs, butter, and cracklins. Pour the batter into the pan and bake for an hour or until the bread is browned on top and a toothpick stuck in the middle comes out clean.
Makes 8 servings.

Hush Puppies

Hush puppies and fried fish are meant for each other. You can make these flat or round, but please do try making them.

1 cup yellow cornmeal
¾ cup all-purpose flour
1½ teaspoons baking power
¼ teaspoon salt
3 large eggs, well beaten
½ cup milk
oil for frying

Heat the oil in a large, heavy skillet. (Cast iron is ideal.) Add the eggs and milk into the dry ingredients and stir until you have a sticky dough. Drop the dough by teaspoons into the hot grease and fry until golden brown. Drain on brown paper.
Makes 6 to 8 servings.

From the Water

The sea that surrounds Beaufort County's beautiful islands offers an abundance for our table.

Oysters Casino

60 oysters on the half shell
60 squares (1 inch each) of lean bacon
10 tablespoons melted butter
1 tablespoon fresh lemon juice
½ cup finely chopped parsley

Preheat the broiler. Each oyster should be loosened but left on the shell. Spread a layer of rock salt over a baking sheet. Arrange the oysters on the salt. Cover each oyster with a square of bacon. Place the baking sheet under the broiler and cook just until the bacon curls and becomes slightly crisp, about 2 minutes. Meanwhile, mix together the butter, lemon juice and parsley. Spoon equal amounts of this mixture onto each oyster. Run the baking sheet under the broiler again just until the butter sizzles.

Lobster Ball

Blend 2 cups of cooked lobster meat with 4 tablespoons melted butter, 1½ teaspoons curry powder, and ¼ teaspoon Worcestershire sauce. Shape spoonfuls of the mixture into small balls. Roll in chopped almonds and chill.

Shrimp or Lobster Cutlets

1 cup milk
1½ tablespoons flour
1 stick butter
salt, hot sauce and sherry to taste
bread crumbs for rolling cutlets
flour for rolling cutlets
1½ pounds of cooked, chopped shrimp or cooked, chopped lobster
(canned seafood can be substituted)
1 egg, beaten
oil for frying

Make a thick cream sauce with the milk, flour, butter, salt and
hot sauce. Add the seafood and a splash or two of sherry. Shape
dollops of the mixture like croquettes, then mash them flat. Dip
them lightly into flour, then egg, then bread crumbs. Fry in deep fat
until golden brown.

My Mother's Stewed Shrimp

2 tablespoons butter
1 tablespoon flour
2 onions, finely chopped
2 pounds peeled shrimp
6 tomatoes (or 1¾ cups canned tomatoes)
1 green pepper, diced
1 cup water
1 teaspoon chopped parsley
1 bay leaf
½ teaspoon garlic salt
salt and pepper to taste

Melt the butter over medium-low heat and add the flour, stirring constantly. Cook until the flour is light brown. Add onions and cook until they're golden. Add the shrimp and take the mixture off the heat to cool just slightly while you add the tomatoes, water, green pepper and seasonings. Cook, stirring frequently, for 10 minutes. Serve over rice.

Fried Shrimp

2 pounds fresh, unpeeled, medium-size shrimp
4 eggs beaten
⅔ cup mayonnaise
3 tablespoons fresh lemon juice
1 teaspoon garlic powder
1⅓ cups Saltine cracker crumbs
1 cup cornflake crumbs
⅓ cup cornmeal
vegetable oil for frying
cocktail sauce

Peel and devein the shrimp, leaving tails intact. Combine eggs, mayonnaise, lemon juice, and garlic powder in a large bowl. Stir the shrimp in this mixture gently, coating each one well. Cover and chill 3 to 4 hours or until you're ready to fry. Combine cracker and cereal crumbs and cornmeal. Remove the shrimp from the marinade and discard the marinade. Dredge shrimp in crumb mixture and press the crumbs onto the shrimp to make them stick. Deep fry the shrimp in hot oil (375 degrees) until they're golden. Drain on paper towels or brown paper. Serve with cocktail sauce. Makes about 4 servings.

How to cook crabs

If you live in South Carolina's lowcountry, you have to know how to cook crabs. Here's how we do it:

Put one inch of water into a pot. Add 2 or 3 tablespoons of vinegar and salt. When the water boils, throw in the crabs. Cook the crabs for 25 or 30 minutes. The vinegar makes the crabs easy to pick. Keep clean crab shells in the refrigerator and serve some of your seafood dishes on them.

Deviled Crabs

4 tablespoons butter
2 tablespoons flour
1 cup milk
1 teaspoon prepared mustard
½ cup bread crumbs, toasted
2 teaspoons lemon juice
1 tablespoon chopped parsley
2 cups crab meat
2 hard-boiled eggs, minced
salt and pepper to taste

Make a rich cream sauce with the butter, flour and milk. Add all the other ingredients, putting in the chunks of crab last. Spoon the mixture onto crab shells and sprinkle with bread crumbs. Bake at 350 degrees for 30 minutes.
Makes about 8 servings.

Down Home Crab Cakes

½ cup mayonnaise
1 egg, beaten
⅓ cup minced green or sweet red pepper
3 tablespoons minced onion
⅓ cup cooked, white corn kernels (optional)
1 teaspoon dry mustard
¼ to ½ teaspoon black pepper
1 pound fresh lump crabmeat, cooked and flaked
about 2 cups fresh bread crumbs or finely crumbled biscuits
2 tablespoons butter
2 tablespoons vegetable oil
tartar sauce

Combine mayonnaise and egg in a large bowl. Mix in the next
five ingredients. Stir in crab and 1 to 1½ cups of the bread crumbs.
You want to stir in just enough to make the mixture hold its shape.
Shape into 8 patties. Coat the patties with remaining bread crumbs.
Heat the butter and oil in a large, heavy skillet. Add the crab cakes
in batches and fry until they're lightly browned on both sides.
Serve with tartar sauce.
Makes 8 servings.

Fried Soft Shell Crabs

1 egg
½ cup milk
½ to 1 cup flour
1 teaspoon baking powder
pinch of salt
fat for frying

Beat egg and milk in one bowl and mix the flour and baking powder in another. Add salt. Dip the crabs in the egg and milk mixture, then in the flour and baking powder mixture. Cover the bottom of a heavy skillet (cast iron is ideal) in about ½ inch of fat and heat the fat to about 375 degrees. Drop in the crabs and fry until golden brown. Serve with tartar sauce.

Shrimp Salad

1 pound shrimp, cooked and diced
2 large stalks celery, minced
1 medium onion, minced
2 hard-boiled eggs, diced
2 tablespoons lemon juice
⅓ cup mayonnaise
1 tablespoon capers

Mix all ingredients and chill. Serve on lettuce.

This freshwater pond looks deceptively serene at sunset. Just out of sight, alligators prowl for birds and fish.

Catfish Baked with Cheese

6 catfish fillets (about 2 pounds)
½ cup Parmesan cheese
¼ cup flour
1 teaspoon paprika
1 egg, lightly beaten
1 tablespoon milk
8 tablespoons melted butter
¼ cup sliced almonds
salt and pepper

Preheat the oven to 350 degrees. Wipe the catfish dry. Mix the eggs and milk in a flat dish, and the cheese, flour, and paprika in another dish. Add salt and pepper to taste to the dry ingredients. Dip the fillets in the egg mixture and then coat them with the cheese mixture. Arrange the fillets in one layer in a baking dish and pour the butter over them. Sprinkle with the almonds. Bake for 20 minutes.
Makes 6 servings.

Hunting Alligators

My cousin Coney loved to hunt alligators. She wasn't afraid to wade barefooted in a pond to find them, either.

Coney would wade into a pond and look around for an alligator half-buried in the mud.

When I was a child, I watched her go after a very old alligator once. As Coney stepped into the pond, that old alligator got completely flat. Coney just kept walking real slow to the gator. She made a noose with a rope and worked it over the alligator's mouth. Then she tightened that noose, and her husband helped her pull the gator out of the water.

They sold the alligator hides and ate the meat.

Cousin Coney put the meat in a pan of water and put in about eight ounces of vinegar. She added four or five fresh garlic cloves and onions and let it all soak for about an hour. Then she took the meat out of the water and rinsed it off. She seasoned it with salt, black pepper, and garlic powder. Then it was ready to bake at 350 degrees for an hour, with lots of onions cut up all over the meat.

Alligator is also good to fry in a pan of hot oil. The legs taste like chicken, and the tail tastes like fish.

Photo by Barbara Martin

A gator dubbed "Big Al" by the locals on Fripp Island suns himself near a pond on the golf course.

Alligator Tail

2 pounds of alligator tail, ground
2 teaspoons salt
1 teaspoon red pepper
1 egg, beaten
¼ cup milk
½ cup bread crumbs
juice of 1 lemon
½ cup onions, chopped
2 tablespoon fresh parsley, chopped
1 cup flour
1 cup cornmeal
fat for deep frying

Mix alligator meat with salt, pepper, egg, milk, crumbs, juice, onions and parsley. Shape into small balls. Mix together the flour and cornmeal, and roll the balls in the mixture to coat them. Fry in deep fat at 350 degrees until the alligator balls are brown.

From the Woods
and Marshes

Photo by Barbara Martin

For local hunters, the abundance of wildlife offers an opportunity for a freezer full of meat. This buck, though, lives on Fripp Island, where he is protected, and he's so tame, he'll take food from your hand.

Venison Roast

1 haunch of venison
½ pound bacon
1 large onion, chopped
salt and pepper to taste

Wash the meat in tepid water and dry thoroughly with a cloth. Toss the chopped onion with salt and pepper. Cut slits in the meat and stuff the onion pieces inside the slits. Cover the venison with bacon strips. Put the venison with 1 cup of water in a large pot, cover, and cook in a low oven, allowing 25 minutes per pound. Baste the meat frequently.

Broiled Squirrel

Squirrel is more succulent and tender than most wild meats. Its flavor is mild, not gamey, if it's cooked right. There is no need for soaking, and most of the time, you don't even have to parboil it. Squirrels should be cleaned as soon as possible after shooting, but skinning can wait until they are about to be cooked.

Clean the squirrel and rub the meat with salt and pepper. Brush it with fat and place it on a hot broiling rack. Broil 40 minutes, turning frequently and basting with drippings every ten minutes. Serve the meat with gravy made from the drippings and season with 1 to 2 tablespoons of lemon juice.

Deep-Fried Quail

Clean quail thoroughly. Salt and flour each bird, then place a lump of butter and a few grains of basil in the cavity. Fry in deep fat. The fat should be hot at first until the bird is brown all over. Then bring the temperature down and cook for about 20 minutes more. Drain on brown paper and serve hot.

Roasted Quail

Clean quail thoroughly. Salt lightly and place a lump of butter inside each bird. Rub bird with a mixture of flour and butter. Place in a baking pan and bake at 300 degrees for about an hour, basting frequently with a little water mixed with melted butter, sherry wine, and ¼ teaspoon of marjoram or tarragon.

Smothered Marsh Hens

Parboil eight skinned birds in salt water just long enough to take out the blood and keep the shape. Drain and put in a deep frying pan on top of the stove. Add the following ingredients to make gravy:

2 cups chicken stock or 1 can of chicken soup
6 tablespoons of flour
6 tablespoons of bacon grease
salt and pepper to taste

Cover and cook about 1 hour, then uncover and slip under the broiler flame for 15 minutes.

Potted Doves

6 doves
6 slices of bacon
1 cup catsup
1 small onion, sliced
3 tablespoons Worcestershire sauce
1 tablespoon butter
red pepper or hot sauce
salt and pepper

Steam birds for 20 minutes on top of the stove with a little water. Then add onion, seasonings, and catsup and lay the bacon on top of the birds. Cook, covered, for about 1½ hours or until the birds are very tender. Remove the cover and brown in the oven.

Wild Duck with Mushrooms

1 duck
1 onion, sliced
½ cup butter or drippings
salt and pepper
2 cups water
1 cup fresh mushrooms, sliced
2 tablespoons flour
pinch of powdered thyme
1 bay leaf

Prepare and disjoint the duck and brown with the onions in the fat.
Add salt and pepper, bay leaf, and the water. Cook 1½ hours on
low heat. In a separate pan, sauté the mushrooms and add flour and
thyme. Add to the duck and continue to cook 30 minutes. Serve the
duck on a chop plate and surround it with wild rice.

From the Pen

Photo by Barbara Martin

My husband, Quitman, feeds our chickens.

Barbecue Chicken

6 chicken breast quarters, skin removed
⅓ cup margarine, melted (optional)
salt and pepper
3 cups of Mama's Barbecue Sauce (recipe follows)

Preheat the oven to 350 degrees. Arrange the chicken breast
quarters in a greased baking pan. Sprinkle with salt and pepper and
brush with margarine, if desired. Cover tightly with tin foil and
bake 1¼ to 1½ hours, or until the meat is tender. Remove the foil.
Pour off drippings and pour hot barbecue sauce over the chicken
just before serving.

Mama's Barbecue Sauce

½ cup water
¼ cup cider vinegar
¼ cup butter or margarine
2 tablespoons sugar
2 tablespoons Worcestershire sauce
1 tablespoon prepared mustard
1½ teaspoons salt
½ teaspoon black pepper
¼ teaspoon red pepper
1 thick slice of lemon
1 thick slice of onion, peeled
½ cup catsup

Combine all ingredients except catsup in a heavy saucepan. Bring
to a boil, stirring frequently. Reduce heat and simmer, partially
covered, for 20 minutes. Remove from heat and discard lemon and
onion slices. Stir in catsup.

Fried Chicken

1 2-pound chicken
1 cup lemon juice
1 teaspoon salt
½ teaspoon black pepper
flour for dredging
oil for frying

Wash and pat chicken dry. Cut into pieces, place in a container and add lemon juice. Cover and refrigerate for 1 hour. Rinse the chicken pieces, pat dry, and season with salt and pepper. Dredge chicken in flour. In a large pot, heat about a half inch of oil. Add chicken pieces and cover. Fry on high heat until the chicken is browned. Reduce heat to medium-low, cover and cook for about 30 minutes. Remove from the heat and drain on brown paper. Serve hot.

Fried Chicken Livers

not worth the effort

There is nothing better than fresh chicken livers. I eat them for breakfast with eggs. I like them with onions, too.

1 pound chicken livers
1 cup buttermilk
1 cup self-rising flour
vegetable oil for frying

Combine livers and buttermilk and let stand 10 minutes. Drain the livers in a colander. Dredge the livers in flour and deep fry in hot oil (350 degrees) for 3 to 4 minutes or until the livers are browned. Drain.

Roasted Pork

Pig time! There's nothing about pork I don't like. What is now being referred to as "the other white meat" has always been plain ol' pork to me, and I have always loved it. One thing with Mr. Pig—you have pig's feet, pig ears, pig tails, pig snouts, pig ribs...You can eat most everything on Mr. Pig, good ol' pork meat.

1 leg pork, 8 to 10 pounds
1 cup brown sugar
1 tablespoon salt
1 tablespoon black pepper
1 quart canned tomatoes
3 sliced onions
1 tablespoon hot sauce
1 cup tomato catsup
1 cup water

Rub the pork with the brown sugar, salt and pepper. Place the pork in a large roasting pan (preferably a double roaster) and add the remaining ingredients. Roast in a 350 degree oven, about 30 minutes per pound.

Hog's Head Cheese

When we killed a hog on our farm, no part of the hog was wasted, including the head. This recipe has been handed down through generations of my family. Our traditional Christmas and New Year's Day breakfast is still hog's head cheese and hominy grits. It is also delicious with crackers.

½ hog's head, cleaned
2 tablespoons allspice
¼ cup vinegar
salt to taste
hot pepper
catsup or hot sauce to taste

Cover the hog's head with water and vinegar and boil until the meat falls off the bone. Reserve the water. Mince the meat fine, removing all the small bones. Take the water the hog's head was boiled in and add to the meat until the mixture has the consistency of thin pudding. Season the mixture and pour in molds. This will congeal into a jelly that can be sliced.

About the Author

Eva Smalls Segar was born in 1937 on a farm in Beaufort County's Dale community. She lives within a stone's throw of the home she grew up in, but she has come a long way from her poor upbringing.

Encouraged by her parents to work hard and believe in God, she was determined to educate herself and find a job helping people.

She graduated from Robert Smalls High School and went on to become a nurse at Beaufort Memorial Hospital in 1973. She retired after more than thirty years at the hospital.

She and her husband, Quitman, own a working farm in Dale. They have two grown children and ten grandchildren.

Mrs. Segar is active in the Jehovah's Witness Kingdom Hall.

Her first book, **Songs to Sing, Stories to Tell: Growing Up Gullah,** was published in 2004 and is in its third printing. Her second book, **More Songs to Sing, Stories to Tell: Growing Up Gullah 2**, was published in 2005.